Wo Bhi Apne Na Hue....

Muskan

BookLeaf Publishing
India | USA | UK

Made with ❤ on the BookLeaf Publishing Platform
www.bookleafpub.in
www.bookleafpub.com

Dedication

उन सभी एहसासों के नाम,
जो शब्दों में ढलने से पहले ही टूट गए।

To all the hearts who feel too deeply,
but speak too little.

Preface

There comes a point in everyone's life when the silence speaks louder than words, when unspoken feelings echo louder than conversations. This book was born in those quiet pauses, in the space between what I felt and what I could say.

Each poem here is a mirror—a reflection of emotions we all carry but rarely articulate. Be it longing, love, anger, or gratitude—these verses are not just mine; they are yours too.

I chose to write in both **Hindi** and **English** not just for wider reach, but to let these emotions breathe in two languages. **Hindi holds the soul**, and **English lends the wings**.

If even one poem feels like your story—my purpose is fulfilled.

— मुस्कान

Acknowledgements

First and foremost, I thank my heart—for feeling enough to write, and my silence—for letting me listen.

To my parents, for teaching me the meaning of love without conditions.

To the ones who came into my life briefly and unknowingly left behind poems.

And lastly, to every reader who holds this book today—thank you for giving my words a home.

Contents

ज़िन्दगी से एक मुलाक़ात

एक रोज़ सुबह, एक मोड़ पर
मैंने कहा, उसे रोक कर –
"हाथ बढ़ा ए ज़िन्दगी,
आंख मिला कर बात कर!"

हर रोज़ तुझे जीने के लिए
एक नई सुबह मिल जाती है।
कोई रात कभी मुरझाती है,
तो कोई शाम मेरी खिल जाती है।

कोई पिछला किस्सा ख़त्म कर
जब नई सुबह तक आती हूँ,
हर बार न जाने खुद को
क्यों एक नए मोड़ पर पाती हूँ।

ख़फ़ा नहीं हूँ तुझसे मैं,
बस कुछ जवाब मैं चाहती हूँ। चल,
हाथ बढ़ा ए ज़िन्दगी,
अब आंख मिला कर बात कर।

A Meeting with Life

One morning, at a turning lane.
I paused and said, not in vain –
"Reach out your hand, O life so still,
Look into my eyes, let's talk at will."
Each day I try to live you right,
A new dawn brings a softer light.
Some nights wither in silent sighs,
But some evenings bloom like sunrise.
I close a chapter from the past,
And by the morning, breathe at last.
Yet every time, without a clue,
I find myself on paths brand new.
I'm not angry with you, my friend,
Just seeking answers that don't pretend.
Come now, extend your hand once more,
Look into my eyes, let your silence pour.

लफ्ज़ों में बसी ज़िंदगी

ज़िंदगी पर एक किताब लिखूंगी,
उसमें सारे हिसाब लिखूंगी।
जितने सवाल अधूरे हैं,
उन सबके उसमें जवाब लिखूंगी।

कुछ बदलते अपनों के लहजे लिखूंगी,
कुछ अपने टूटे ख़्वाब लिखूंगी।
खुलकर कभी जो कह न सकी,
वो सारे अपने जज़्बात लिखूंगी।

जो ज़ख़्म दिए हैं अपनों ने,
उन सबके झूठे राज़ लिखूंगी।अपने हर दर्द की आवाज़ लिखूंगी,
दिल की सारी बात लिखूंगी।
ज़िंदगी पर एक किताब लिखूंगी,
उसमें सारे हिसाब लिखूंगी।

Life Inked in Words

I'll write a book on life one day,
Where all my debts and dues will lay.
Each question left without reply,
Will find its answer, no more why.
I'll pen the tones that loved ones changed,
And shattered dreams, so sadly arranged.
The truths I never dared to share,
Will bleed as feelings, laid out bare.
The wounds my dearest ones have made,
Their hidden lies I won't let fade.
Each hurt I've held, each silent cry,
Will find its voice — no need to hide.
Yes, I'll write a book on life someday,
Where every score is marked my way.

आग जैसा इश्क़

नर्म लफ्ज़ों में लिपटी
एक बेचैन सी तासीर,
जो छूते ही जला दे
और जला कर भी
खुद को सौंप दे।
इश्क़ –
जो सर्द रातों में
अंदर तक सेंक दे,
और फिर भी
बाहर से ख़ामोश रहे।
वो इश्क़...
ना बुझ सके,
ना संभल सके,
ना निभ सके –
बस बचे
आग जैसा इश्क़

To Love Like Fire

If you must love, then love with flame,
Let her troubled heart make you restless by name.
If her eyes well up, be her handkerchief tight,
Be the voice to her silence, her calm in the night.
If her sleep is lost, may dreams forsake you too,
If her day goes wrong, let your evenings dim through.
Let her win sometimes, let yourself fall behind,
In her growing innocence, be the scandal they find.
If love is your path, walk it in a daze,
Lose all sense—be the ash in love's blazing blaze

इश्क का आखिरी मकाम – तू

तू इश्क़ कर रहा है तो शिद्दत से कर,
उसकी हालत ठीक न हो तो बेचैन तू हो जा।

आंखें हों नम उसकी , तो रूमाल तू बन जा,
उसकी हर खामोशी की , जुबान तू हो जा।

अगर नींद उसकी उड़े , तो सपने तुझे न आएं,
उसका दिन बुरा हो , तो शामें तेरी घटें।

कभी उसे जीतने दे, और कभी खुद हार जा,
उसके बचपने में तू ही बदनाम हो जा।

अब इश्क़ कर ही रहा है तो पूरे होश से कर,
वरना इस इश्क की आग में तू राख होजा।

The Final Destination of Love – You

If you're falling in love, then do it right,
When they're not okay, let your soul lose its light.
If tears fill their eyes, be the handkerchief near,
Be the voice of their silence, the shield from all fear.
If sleep escapes them, may dreams leave you too,
If their day feels heavy, may your evenings dim blue.
Let them win sometimes, even if you fall,
Be blamed for their mischiefs – absorb it all.
If you've chosen to love, then love with might,
Or let love turn you to ashes in the night.

मोहब्बत नहीं, साथ चाहिए

सुनो,
मेरे थोड़ा क़रीब आ सकते हो क्या?
इस ज़माने से मुझे तुम, बचा सकते हो क्या?

इश्क़ या मोहब्बत नहीं चाहिए मुझे...
पर दोस्ती का हाथ, बढ़ा सकते हो क्या?

यहां भीड़ है बहुत पर, कोई अपना नहीं है...
मुझे इस भीड़ की घुटन से, बचा सकते हो क्या?
बताओ,
मेरे थोड़ा क़रीब आ सकते हो क्या?

Stay – That's Enough

Tell me,
Can you come a little closer to me?
Can you save me from this ruthless world, maybe?
I don't need love or grand desire,
But can you offer friendship that won't expire?
There's a crowd here, bustling and wide,
Yet not one soul feels like mine beside.
This suffocating crowd – can you pull me free?
Tell me...
Can you just come a little closer to me?

तुमसे मोहब्बत के बाद

चेहरे पर ख़ुशी छा जाती है
आँखों में सुरूर आ जाता है
जब तुम मुझे अपना कहते हो
अपने पे ग़ुरूर आ जाता है ।

जब तुमसे मोहब्बत की हमने
तब जा के कहीं ये राज़ खुला
मरने का सलीका आते ही
जीने में सुकून आ जाता है ।

After I Loved You

Joy spreads across my face
A trance lights up my gaze
When you call me yours so true
A pride in myself starts to raise
When I fell in love with you
That's when the truth began to shine
The moment I learned how to die
Living became a peace divine.

हवाओं में तेरी मौजूदगी

"फिर ढल रहा है दिन, फिर शाम हो रही है,
फिर ये कोशिशें कुछ कहने को नाकाम हो रही हैं।

एक लंबे अर्से बाद कुछ सुनाने को दिल किया,
फिर अंदाज़ तेरा ख़ास और नज़्में मेरी आम हो रही हैं।

बाहर शोर ना हो जाए, सो आंखों को ख़ामोश रखा है,
बिन मिलाए नज़रें भी, बातें सरेआम हो रही हैं।

तुम हट जाओ रास्ते से, ना मुड़ो मेरी ओर,
मौजूदगी तुम्हारी मेरी तबाही का इल्ज़ाम हो रही है।

ज़रा संभल के रहना इश्क़ की बर्बादियों से तुम,
मैं तो आज भी मैं हूँ,
मगर मोहब्बत सारी आज भी तेरे नाम हो रही है।"

Your Presence in Air

The day fades again, the dusk returns,
And yet my words still fail and burn.
After a long silence, I longed to speak,
But your tone's still rare, and my poems weak.
I keep my eyes hushed, lest the world hears,
Even without glances, the truth appears.
Step aside—don't turn to see,
Your presence alone is destroying me.
Tread carefully in love's ruins, my dear,
I am still myself, always near—
But every ounce of love today,
Still whispers your name in every way.

वो घर नहीं रहा

बिछड़ कर खुद से वो किधर जाता है,
जब इंसान वो पत्तों की तरह बिखर जाता है।

रूठ कर जहां से कोई जाता है घर
जो कहीं का नहीं रहता वो किधर जाता है?

अपने वजूद पर हमेशा उठाता है उंगलियाँ,
कोई शख़्स जब जीता नहीं ना मर पाता है।

कुछ परिंदों-सी फ़ितरत हो गई है इंसान की,
पर निकलते ही वो घर छोड़ उड़ जाता है ।
आधी उम्र देखे हो अंधेरे जिसने, अचानक से देखे रौशनी
– तो डर जाता है।

Its No longer a home

Where does he go, once parted from his soul,
A man who shatters like dry leaves as a whole?
He storms away from what once was "home,"
Now belongs nowhere—just destined to roam.
He raises doubts on his very existence,
Half-alive, yet denied death's persistence.
A spirit like birds – so restless, so free,
Takes flight the moment he's meant to be.
One who's spent half a life in the dark,
Is startled by light, like a long-lost spark.

उसके जाने के बाद

बेशक तेरी ज़िंदगी में , आज बदलाव दिख रहा है।
पर तेरी बातों में आज भी छुपा एक घाव दिख रहा है।

लाख दावे कर रहे हो तुम उसे भुला देने के , पर तेरी आँखों में उसके लिए लगाव दिख रहा है।

सच जानती है दुनिया, फिर भी छुपा रहे हो,
जाने किसका ये तुम पर, दबाव दिख रहा है।

तुम कहते हो कि खुश हो बिना उसके ज़िंदगी में,
फिर ये चेहरे पर तुम्हारे, कैसा तनाव दिख रहा है?

After He Left

Your life, no doubt, shows signs of change,
a new wind in your step, a shift in your range.
Yet your words still carry a hidden pain, a wound unsaid,
but not in vain.
You claim you've left that love behind,
but your eyes still search, still bind.
The world knows the truth you try to hide,
whose pressure is this—eating you inside?
You say you're happy without him in your life,
then why does your face wear this silent strife?

खुदसे नज़रे मिला कर तो देखो

हाल खराब हैं तो, सुधार क्यों नहीं लेते ,
खुद से ज़िंदगी थोड़ी, उधार क्यों नहीं लेते ।

तुमसे बेहतर कोई जानता होगा क्या तुम्हे ?
तो फिर बात मेरी ये, मान क्यों नहीं लेते ।

घेरे से निकल अपने, ज़रा सा बाहर आके देख
आइने में ज़रा खुदसे नज़रे मिलाके देख ।

ढूंढ तुझमें क्या है , चाहता है तू आखिर क्या ?
खोई हुई इज़्ज़त खुदको वापिस लौटा कर देख ।

बोझ लिए बैठे हो , तो बोझ उतार क्यों नहीं देते
खुद से ज़िंदगी थोड़ी, उधार क्यों नहीं लेते ।

You, Undiscovered

If things are broken, why not fix them now?
Life isn't a loan—so why live it somehow?
Who knows you better than you do inside?
Then why not trust what I confide?
Step out a little, leave that shell...
Look in the mirror, face yourself well.
What is it you seek, what do you desire?
Reclaim your pride, reignite that fire.
You carry burdens, so why not let them fall?
Life isn't borrowed—own it after all.

मैं तुम्हे बचाना चाहती हूं

तुम झूठ बोलते हो अकसर
कि ठीक हो तुम।
मैं तुम्हें हक़ीक़त से मिलना चाहती हूं।

बहुत जल गए हो तुम इस धूप में,
मैं बारिश की पहली बूंद बनकर
तुम्हारी आग बुझाना चाहती हूं।

ये जो निशान पड़ गए हैं किरदार पर तुम्हारे,
एक-एक क़तरे को अपने हाथ से मिटाना चाहती हूं।
बहुत बड़े हो गए हो तुम इस दुनिया के लिए,
मैं तो तुम्हें छोटे बच्चे की तरह अपनी गोद में सुलाना चाहती हूं।

तुम ढूंढो मुझे मेरे बाद भी कहीं,
मैं तुम्हें इस ख़याल तक अपनाना बनाना चाहती हूं।
मैंने सुना है मर्दों को रोना मना है सरेआम,
तुम सिर रखो मेरे कंधे पर,
मैं तुम्हारे आँसू पी जाना चाहती हूं।

तुम झूठ बोलते हो अकसर

कि ठीक हो तुम।
तुम हाथ पकड़ो मेरा,
मैं तुम्हें तुम से बचाना चाहती हूं।
तुम डूब रहे हो, प्रिय –
मैं बस तुम्हें बचाना चाहती हूं।

I Want to Save You

You often lie,
Saying you're fine.
But I want to introduce you to the truth.
You've burned too long in this sun,
And I–
I want to be the first drop of rain
To put out your fire.
Those scars that stain your soul,
I want to wipe each one
With my bare hands.
You've grown too big for this world,
I just want to cradle you like a child,
Let you rest on my lap.
If you ever search for me after I'm gone,
Know this–
I want to live in that thought
You call yourself.
They say men aren't allowed to cry in public,
But rest your head on my shoulder–
Let me drink your tears.

You often lie,
Saying you're fine.
Just hold my hand once,
I want to save you from yourself.
You're drowning, my love—
And all I want is to save you.

तेख़ाने में दीवाने

अकल से ही जो सारे काम लेंगे
दुनिया में कहां फिर दीवाने मिलेंगे।

ये जो बाहर से दिखती है झोपड़ी दिल की
अंदर ना जाने कितने तहखाने मिलेंगे।

जहां बहकने के लिए पीने की ज़रूरत नहीं
यहां तुम्हे ऐसे भी खूबसूरत खज़ाने मिलेंगे।

Love Locked Below

If every step is ruled by mind alone,
Where will the mad, wild hearts be known?
This heart may seem like a fragile hut outside,
But deep within—how many chambers hide?
Where you don't need wine just to lose control,
Even silence here can intoxicate your soul.
There lie treasures—raw, tender, and bright,
In these secret vaults, away from sight.

मोहब्बत की वो नौबत

हम चाहते ही नहीं कि मोहब्बत हो जाए।
हम –
चाहते ही नहीं कि मोहब्बत हो जाए।
जो होगी मोहब्बत तो चेहरे पर उदासी छाएगी,
जो छाएगी उदासी तो तुझे नींद न आएगी।

नींद न आई, तो चेहरे पर असर दिखेगा,
असर आएगा तो तू नज़रे चुराएगा।
और न जाने कब तलक,
और –
न जाने कब तलक
तुम हमसे मिलने नहीं आएगा।

और तू आए न हमसे मिलने,
ऐसी नौबत ही क्यों आए?
तो हम चाहते ही नहीं कि मोहब्बत हो जाए।

That State of Love

We never really wish to fall in love...
No,
We never truly want love to rise above.
Because love brings sadness to the face,
And sadness steals sleep without a trace.
When sleep is gone, the eyes will tell,
And your silence—will speak too well.
You'll start to look away, avoid my gaze,
And distance will stretch across the days...
Who knows then how long you'll stay away?
And why must it come to that anyway?
So, no—
We never truly wish for love to find its way.

मैंने उसे जाने दिया

मैंने उसे जाने दिया...
बिलकुल वैसे ही, जैसे पतझड़ में पत्ते पेड़ों से खुद को अलग कर देते हैं,
बिना शिकायत, बिना किसी वज़ह के पूछे

मैंने उसे जाने दिया ।

जब मेरा नाम उसकी आवाज़ में हल्का पड़ने लगा
जब मेरी मौजूदगी उसके लिए बस एक आदत लगने लगी

मैंने उसे जाने दिया ।

उसे रोकने की चीख को अपनी ज़ुबान पर कैद कर
उसकी आंखों में अपने प्रति कुछ न देख कर
जब मेरे पैरों तले ज़मीन खिसकने लगी

तो एक लंबी सांस लेकर , आंसू भीतर रखकर
मैंने उसे जाने दिया ।

I Let Him Go

I let him go...
Just like autumn leaves
Detach from trees,
Without protest,
Without asking why.
I let him go,
When my name lost weight in his voice,
When my presence
Became no more than a habit he wore.
I let him go,
Swallowing the scream that begged him to stay,
Finding nothing left in his eyes
That once saw only me.
When the ground beneath me began to slip,
And love turned into quiet ache—
I took a long breath,
Buried the tears inside,
And softly...
I let him go.

हम और हमारे बीच

जब इश्क़ रहे पर बातें कम हों
जब अपना बस अकेलापन हो
जब सीने में बेहद ग़म हो
जब रात में आँखें भी नम हों...!!

समझ लेना... कुछ टूट रहा है,
जब साँसें सिर्फ नाम को चलें
जब ज़हन में हो बस सवाल भरे
जब उस पर कोई जवाब न हो
जब घुट-घुट कर तुम रोज़ रोओ...!!

समझ लेना.. क़ुछ टूट रहा है,
जब नज़रें खे परज़ुबान नही
जब साथ में रहना सज़ा लगे....!!

जब मायूस तो पर खो नहीं
जब रोज़ लड़ो पर मरो नहीं
समझ लेना... कुछ टूट रहा है,
एक रिश्ता है जो रूठ रहा है...!!

The Quiet Undoing

When love is there but talks grow few...
When all you have is solitude...!!
When your chest holds endless pain...
When eyes at night are wet with rain...!!
Understand... something's breaking,
When breaths are just in name taken...
When mind is filled with endless questions...!!
When there's no answer or direction...
When every day you weep in suppression...!!
Understand... something's breaking,
When eyes can't speak their silent plea...
When being together feels like penalty...!!
When you're sad but never lost...
When you fight daily but don't exhaust...!!
Understand... something's breaking,
A bond is fading, quietly aching...!!

कोई खास नहीं

सुनो...
जब दुनिया पूछे कौन हूँ मैं...?
तुम कह देना कोई खास नहीं ।

एक दोस्त थी पक्की कच्ची सी
एक डोर थी आधी सच्ची सी
थी ऐसी साथी जीवन की
अब जो पास होकर भी पास नहीं
कोई तुमसे पूछे कौन हूँ मैं...?
तुम कह देना कोई खास नहीं ।

वो रहती तो थी साथ मेरे
पर उसमें थी वो बात नहीं
वो चेहरा है मेरी यादों में
पर अब उसके लिए कोई जज़्बात नहीं ।

वो पास थी दिल के पहले मेरे
पर अब वो मुझको रास नहीं
क्यूंकि अब वो इतनी खास नहीं ।

No One Special

Listen...
When the world asks, who am I?
You say, no one special, no lie...
There was a friend, steadfast yet fragile...
A thread...
Half true, half fragile...
A companion of life's mile...
Now close, yet miles apart...
If someone asks you, who am I?
You say, no one special, just a sigh...
She stayed close once by my side...
But something was missing deep inside...
Her face lingers in my memories' sea...
But no emotions now remain for she...
She was close to my heart's core...
But now she fits me no more...
Because now she's not that special anymore.

कभी हुआ है ऐसा ?

कभी हुआ है ऐसा?
कि खुश हो तुम, पर बाहर से...
परेशान हो, अपनी चाहत से...
शांति है चेहरे पर,
पर मरते हो घबराहट से...!!!

कभी हुआ है ऐसा?
कि दुखी नहीं हो,
पर रोना चाहो राहत से...
जब तूफ़ान मचा हो सीने में,
और मज़ा न हो उस जीने में...
दिन तुम्हारे रोज़ ढले,
पर नींद न हो उस सोने में...!!!

कभी हुआ है ऐसा?
कि तुम चाहो,
कहना सबकुछ लोगों से...
पर बची कोई उम्मीद न हो अब,
ऐसे अपने "ग़ैरों" से...!!

Has It Ever Happened ?

Has it ever happened—
That you smile, yet deep inside you ache,
You're calm outside, but inside you break,
Your face shows peace, serene, so still,
But panic eats you against your will?
Has it ever been—
You're not sad, but wish to cry,
Longing for relief, though you don't know why,
A storm inside, the silence loud,
Life feels dull beneath the cloud.
Days pass by, the nights do too,
But sleep escapes, it won't come through...
And has it ever been—
You long to pour your heart to some,
But even hope has now grown numb.
And all that's left to say or share,
Feels wasted on those once who cared.

एक जाती हुई औरत

एक जाती हुई औरत
ले जाती है अपने साथ अतीत के चुम्बन,
पश्चात्ताप से भरी तुम्हारी आत्मा के अश्रु –

और पीछे छोड़ देती है
वे सभी दुःस्वप्न
जो प्रेम के नाम पर उसने समेट लिये थे।
तुम कभी नहीं जान सकोगे
जाते हुए उसकी आँखें नम थीं या नहीं।

अब तुम्हारी ओर उसका हृदय नहीं –
उसकी जाती हुई पीठ है।

A Woman Who Walked Away

A woman who walks away
Carries with her the kisses of the past.
The tears of your soul soaked in regret –
And leaves behind
All the nightmares
She had gathered in love's name.
You'll never know
If her eyes were moist as she left.
Her heart no longer faces you –
Only her fading back remains.

तुम कम मत होना

याद रखना

वो कहेंगे –

कम बोलो,

कम खाओ,

कम सजो,

कम घूमो,

कम हँसो, खिलखिलाओ,

कम बनाओ दोस्त,

कम करो सपने,

कम हो,

रहो कम।

मेरी दोस्त!

तुम कम सुनना।

Hear Them Less

Remember

They'll say –

Speak less,

Eat less,

Dress less,

Roam less,

Laugh less, burst out less,

Make fewer friends,

Dream smaller dreams,

Be less,

Always be... less.

But my friend –

You – hear them less.

हँसी की तलाश में

चलो हँसने की कोई
हम वजह ढूंढते हैं,
जिधर न हो कोई ग़म
वो जगह ढूंढते हैं।

चलते-चलते बहुत थक गए हैं,
अब इस आसमान के नीचे
कहीं छाँव ढूंढते हैं।

जहाँ खुश रहें हम
ऐसी जगह ढूंढते हैं,
बहुत रो लिए इन अंधेरों में,
चलो इनमें छुपी एक सुबह ढूंढते हैं।

In Search of Smiles

Let's find a reason to smile again,
A place untouched by sorrow or pain.
We've walked too long, too far, too low,
Let's find a shade where peace may grow.
Let's search a place where hearts can rest,
A quiet shelter, soft and blessed.
We've cried enough in nights so deep,
Let's find the dawn these shadows keep.

मुझे अच्छा लगेगा

मैं तो आई हूँ कई बार
तेरी बनाई हदों के पार
अपने प्रेम के पुल से।
एक बार जो तू भी मिलने की इच्छा जताए –
तो मुझे अच्छा लगेगा।
मैंने तो निभाए हैं
तेरे गढ़े सब अनुबंध, प्रतिबंध
तेरे प्रेम को पाने के लिए।
तू भी कभी
प्रेम की रीत निभाए –
तो मुझे अच्छा लगेगा।
मैं जो जताऊँ और बताऊँ
वो तो ख़ूब समझता है तू,
कभी जो तू मेरी ख़ामोशी पढ़ पाए –
तो मुझे अच्छा लगेगा।
तेरी एक शिकन पर
गुज़रता है मेरा पूरा दिन फ़िक्र में,
तेरी बातों में भी
कभी जो मेरा ज़िक्र आए –
मुझे अच्छा लगेगा।

हर कोई कहता रहता है मुझे
तेरे प्रेम में कितनी दीवानी हूँ मैं,
कभी तू भी मेरे प्रेम में
दीवाना कहलाए –
तो मुझे अच्छा लगेगा।

It Would Make Me Happy

I've crossed your boundaries
More than once –
Walking on bridges built from my love.
If you'd ever express the wish to meet –
It would make me happy.
I've honored all your crafted rules and restrictions
Just to be worthy of your love.
If you could follow even a single ritual of love –
It would make me happy.
You always understand what I say and show,
But if you could once read my silence –
It would make me happy.
One crease on your forehead
Consumes my whole day in worry.
If ever in your words
You mentioned me –
It would make me happy.
Everyone says
How madly I love you,
But if one day,

You're called mad in love with me –

It would make me happy.

मैं नहीं तो कोई और होगा

मैं नहीं तो कोई और होगा,
तेरी मुस्कान में एक नया शोर होगा।
वक़्त रुकता नहीं किसी की रज़ा से,
तेरे ख्वाबों में अब कोई और चाँद-सा गौर होगा।

जिसे मैं समझी था अपने हिस्से की राहत,
वो किसी और की अब आदत-सी होगी।
जिस बात पर मैं ठहर गयी थी,
वो बात किसी और के लिए रवायत होगी।

मैंने जो पन्ने अधूरे छोड़े थे,
शायद अब वो कोई और लिखेगा।
मेरे बिना भी ये कहानी चलेगी,
किसी और का नाम तेरी ज़ुबां पे दिखेगा।
तेरी राहों में अब कोई और मोड़ होगा।
वो मैं नहीं तो कोई और होगा।

If Not Me, Then Someone Else

If not me, then someone else will be,
A new spark in your smile, wild and free.
Time bows to no one's plea or grace,
Another moon-like glow will take my place.
What I once thought was my peace to hold,
Is now someone else's habit, quietly bold.
The words where I paused and stayed behind,
Will now be rituals for another to find.
The pages I left incomplete in pain,
Someone else will finish them, line by line again.
This story will go on without my name,
Your lips will still speak – just not the same.
On your path now, someone else will glow.
If not me... then someone else will be.

वो मेरे इश्क का दौर था

वो मेरे इश्क का दौर था

वो मेरी धड़कनों का शोर था,
हर लम्हा बस उसी का ज़ोर था।
उसकी हँसी में शाम ढलती थी,
उसकी नज़र में रात मचलती थी।

वो जब भी पास आता था,
दिल बेवजह मुस्काता था।
वो कुछ कहे तो क्या बात थी,
ना कहे , तो भी उसमें कुछ तो बात थी।
अब यादें रह गईं उस दौर की,
जिसमें बस खुशबू थी तेरे होने की।
कभी था जो साँसों के बराबर

वो मेरे इश्क़ का दौर था।

It Was an Era Of My Love

He was the rhythm in my every beat,
A pull so strong, it felt complete.
His laughter softened the evening skies,
His gaze made the silent moonrise.
Whenever he came a little close,
My heart would bloom like a hidden rose.
If he spoke – it was poetry in air.
If he didn't – still, the silence would stare.
Now memories linger from that time,
When his presence felt like a rhyme.
The scent of him still gently stays,
In corners of long-forgotten days.
Once he was my every breath,
That was the era my heart had left.
That was the era... when I loved him best

तुम मुझे माफ़ कर पाओगे ना ?

तुम मुझे माफ़ कर पाओगे ना?
जब वक्त की आँधियाँ सब कुछ बहा ले जाएँगी,
और मेरी आवाज़ बस यादों में रह जाएगी।
जब मेरी गलती तुम्हारी नींदों में काँटे बन जाएगी,
क्या तब भी तुम्हारे दिल में मेरी कुछ जगह रह जाएगी?

मैंने लफ्ज़ों से जो ज़ख्म दिए, वो नासूर न बन जाएँ,
मैं डरती हूँ कहीं मेरी खामोशी तुम्हें और ना तड़पाए।
जो नहीं कहा, वो भी भारी है, जो कह दिया वो कुछ कम नहीं,
पर हर एक लम्हे में मेरा पछतावा चुपचाप शामिल है।
तुम जब अपनी आँखें बंद करोगे,
क्या मेरी सूरत एक अफ़सोस बनकर नही उभरेगी?

क्या तुम्हारा दिल मेरी गलतियों को धड़कनों से अलग कर पाएगा?
क्या माफ़ी का वो पल तुम्हारे सीने में कोई राहत ला पाएगा?
मैं नहीं जानती,
पर एक यही सवाल हर रात मेरा हृदय से पूछता है –
"तुम मुझे माफ़ कर पाओगे ना?"

Will You be able to Forgive Me ?

Will you ever forgive me,
When time's storm washes all traces away,
And my voice survives only as a whisper
Caught in the corners of yesterday?
When my mistakes
Turn into thorns in your sleepless nights,
Will a part of your heart
Still hold me in soft, aching light?
The wounds my words may have carved,
I pray they don't linger as scars.
I fear – what if my silence
Tears you apart more than the wars?
What I never said still weighs like stone,
And what I did... that pain's not alone.
In every unspoken moment,
My quiet regret had deeply grown.
And when you close your eyes someday,
Will my face return as a shadow of sorrow?
Can your heart ever separate my faults

From the love we tried to borrow?
Can that one breath of forgiveness
Bring you peace, even if I'm gone?
I don't know.
But each night, my soul still trembles and asks –
"Will you be able to forgive me?"

अब कोई और नहीं चाहिए

अब कोई और नहीं चाहिए

बस अब कोई और नहीं चाहिए
बस अब कोई और नहीं चाहिए,
तेरे बाद कोई और कहानी नहीं चाहिए।
जिसमें तू था, वहीं तक ठीक था,
उससे आगे कोई नई रवानी नहीं चाहिए।

तेरी यादें ही काफी हैं साँसों के लिए,
अब किसी और की मेहरबानी नहीं चाहिए।
जो अधूरा था, उसे अधूरा ही रहने दे,
इश्क़ में अब कोई नई निशानी नहीं चाहिए।
बहुत थक चुकी हूँ समझाकर दिल को,
अब कोई नज़दीकी, कोई जवानी नहीं चाहिए।

जिसने तोड़ दिया, उसी से जुड़ी हूँ अब भी,
इस पागलपन की अब नयी कहानी नहीं चाहिए।
तू अगर लौटे, तो भी बिना आवाज़ के आना,
अब शोर में कोई भी पुरानी परेशानी नहीं चाहिए।

बस बैठ जाना पास चुपचाप, वही काफी होगा,
अब तकरार, सवाल, या जवाबी नहीं चाहिए।

No One Else, Not Anymore

No one else, not anymore –
After you, I seek no new lore.
Where you once were, that place feels right,
Beyond that, I need no new light.
Your memories breathe within my chest,
I don't need another's kindness to rest.
What was left incomplete, let it remain so,
In love, I crave no newer glow.
I've grown tired of calming my soul,
No new nearness, no passion, no role.
I'm still tied to the one who broke me down,
No new madness in love I'll crown.
And if you ever find your way back to me,
Come quietly – let it just be.
No echoes, no noise, no old melodies,
Just sit beside me...
That will be enough, finally.

आहिस्ता चल ऐ ज़िंदगी

आहिस्ता चल ऐ ज़िंदगी...
कुछ कर्ज़ चुकाने बाकी हैं,
कुछ दर्द मिटाने बाकी हैं,
कुछ फ़र्ज़ निभाने बाकी हैं...!

कुछ रिश्ते हैं जो रूठ गए,
रूठों को मनाना बाकी है,
रोतों को हँसाना बाकी है...!

कुछ हसरतें अभी अधूरी हैं,
कुछ काम बहुत ज़रूरी हैं...
ख़्वाहिशें घुटी हैं जो दिल में,
उनको दफ़नाना बाकी है...!

आहिस्ता चल ऐ ज़िंदगी...
कुछ ज़ख़्म छुपाने बाकी हैं...!!

Pause Your Pace Life

Stay a little longer, life...
Some debts are yet to be repaid,
Some tears are waiting to fade,
Some duties still await the aid...
Some bonds broke and drifted away,
Some left without a word to say,
The hurt ones still need to hear our call,
And those who weep—deserve to laugh after all...
Some dreams remain only half-spun,
Some tasks must still be done.
Some wishes choke quietly inside the heart,
They too must be buried, given a part...
Stay a little longer, life...
Some wounds still need to be veiled tonight.

सबके हिस्से में नहीं आता

ये ज़मीं, ये आसमान
ये ख़ुशी, ये मुस्कान
रोटी, कपड़ा और मकान –
सबके हिस्से में नहीं आता।
ये ऐतबार, ये प्यार,
ये आँसू, ये इंतज़ार,
सुकून भरा एक इतवार –
सबके हिस्से में नहीं आता।
ये मंज़िल, ये रास्ता,
ये सफर, ये रात, ये शाम, ये सहर,
हाथ पकड़ के चले – वो हमसफ़र
सबके हिस्से में नहीं आता।
बेशक ये किसी कहानी, किसी क़िस्से में नहीं आता –
कि ज़िंदगी मिलती है,
मगर जीना सबके हिस्से में नहीं आता।

Not in Everyone's Share

This earth, this sky,
This joy, this smile,
Food, clothes, a roof –
Are not in everyone's share.
This trust, this love,
These tears, this wait,
A peaceful Sunday –
Are not in everyone's share.
This destination, this path,
This journey, this night, this dusk, this dawn,
To walk hand in hand – that companion
Is not in everyone's share.
Surely, it's not found in tales or lore –
That though we are given life,
To truly live... is not in everyone's share.

रोज़ का तमाशा

काली अंधेरी रात में यादें निकली हैं
दिल की सुनी गलियों में
तमाशा करने को।
कौन समझाए इनको –
ये सिरफिरी और बहकी हुई हैं।
सारी रात भटकेंगी यूं ही
दिल के चप्पे-चप्पे को
रौंदते हुए पैरों तले।
रोज़ का तमाशा है।
मगर अफ़सोस –
इस दिल को
ये सब सहने की
ज़रा भी तो आदत नहीं।
दिल का ये दर्द
नासूर हो चला है।
नींद आएगी नहीं –
रोज़ का सिलसिला है।

The Daily Spectacle

On dark, black nights, memories rise,
Roaming the lonely alleys of my heart
To stage their cruel spectacle.
Who will explain to them?
They are wild – reckless and lost.
All night they'll wander like this,
Crushing every inch of my heart
Beneath their feet.
It's a daily performance.
But alas –
This heart,
It hasn't learned
To endure any of this.
This pain of the heart
Has turned into a wound that never heals.
Sleep will not come –
It's the same story every night.

सवाल सिर्फ मुझसे क्यों ?

मैं क्या चाहती हूं?
मुझे क्या चाहिए?
मेरे लिए क्या सही है?
मुझे क्या करना चाहिए?
मैंने जो किया वो सही था या नहीं?
मैं ज़्यादा तो नहीं बोल रही हूं?
मेरे बारे में ये सब तय करने का हक़ मुझे क्यों नहीं?
और अगर है – तो फिर मैं मतलबी कैसे?
इतने सवाल सिर्फ मुझसे ही क्यों?
क्या इन सवालों की ज़िम्मेदार भी मैं ही हूं – और आप नहीं?

Questions, Always at My Door

What do I want?
What do I need?
What is right for me?
What should I really do?
Was what I did right or not?
Am I speaking too much?
Why don't I have the right to decide all this for myself?
And if I do – then how am I selfish?
Why are all these questions only for me?
Am I the only one responsible for them – and not you?

अंत का अर्थ

मृत्यु जब दस्तक देती है
तो महज़ इंसान नहीं मरता।

फिर मरती है –
उससे की हुई मोहब्बत,
उससे जुड़े हुए रिश्ते,
उसके लौट आने की उम्मीद,
उसके साथ गए शिकवे,
और कुछ समय बाद –
उसका व्यक्तित्व।

"अंतः तुमसे जुड़े रहने के लिए
मेरा अंत निश्चित है।"

When Death Knocks

When death knocks,
It isn't just a person who dies.
Then also dies –
The love once shared with them,
The relationships tied to them,
The hope of their return,
The complaints that left with them,
And after some time –
Even their identity.
"In the end,
To stay connected to you,
My end is inevitable."

About the Author

Muskan Sharma,

from Delhi's streets and solitude's quiet corners,
writes not just to express – but to survive.
What began five years ago as tear-stained pages,
now breathes as her first book – a whisper made visible.
Her poems don't speak loudly.
They sit beside you –
in heartbreak, healing, and silent nights.

"Some write to be heard, she writes to breathe."

"नज़दीक-ए-दिल है, हर लफ़्ज़।"

(Each word, close to the heart.)

She believes words carry weight –
enough to lift even the heaviest soul.